LAND OF FIRE

PREVIOUS WINNERS OF THE DORSET PRIZE

Ice, Mouth, Song by Rachel Contreni Flynn
Selected by Stephen Dunn

Red Summer by Amaud Jamaul Johnson
Selected by Ray Gonzalez

Dancing in Odessa by Ilya Kaminsky
Selected by Eleanor Wilner

Dismal Rock by Davis McCombs
Selected by Linda Gregerson

Biogeography by Sandra Meek
Selected by the Tupelo Press Editors

Archicembalo by G. C. Waldrep
Selected by C. D. Wright

Severance Songs by Joshua Corey
Selected by Ilya Kaminsky

After Urgency by Rusty Morrison
Selected by Jane Hirshfield

domina Un/blued by Ruth Ellen Kocher
Selected by Lynn Emanuel

Into Daylight by Jeffrey Harrison
Selected by Tom Sleigh

The Well Speaks of Its Own Poison by Maggie Smith
Selected by Kimiko Hahn

One Hundred Hungers by Lauren Camp
Selected by David Wojahn

Almost Human by Thomas Centolella
Selected by Edward Hirsch

MARIO
CHARD

LAND OF FIRE

Tupelo Press
North Adams, Massachusetts

Land of Fire.

Library of Congress Cataloging-in-Publication Data available upon request.
ISBN: 978-1-946482-09-9

Cover and text designed by Josef Beery. Text composed in Electra.

First edition: March 2018.

Tupelo Press
P.O. Box 1767, North Adams, Massachusetts 01247
(413) 664-9611 / editor@tupelopress.org / www.tupelopress.org

Tupelo Press is an award-winning independent literary press that publishes fine fiction, nonfiction, and poetry in books that are a joy to hold as well as read. Tupelo Press is a registered 501(c)(3) nonprofit organization, and we rely on public support to carry out our mission of publishing extraordinary work that may be outside the realm of the large commercial publishers. Financial donations are welcome and are tax deductible.

For my parents

CONTENTS

WE MAKE A THING WE MARVEL

We make a thing we marvel
and learn to worry.

Light
through the red glass of a prophet's robe
makes us red.

We see a horse return the hour before storm
in distress.

We distress.

The thing we make
learns to marvel light.

We think worry is a robe
we can outgrow.

In the mirror we see our bodies without robes
distressed.

It storms.

The prophet marvels at the horse
that spoke.

LAND OF FIRE

up they rose
As from unrest, and each the other viewing,
Soon found their eyes how opened, and their minds
How darkened.

—PARADISE LOST

the animals are not suspicious. The doe
twice beguiled by a fox to enter the lion's den
can speak but does not at death say
I was suspicious.

Hiking to Prophet's Rock we join a company
of gnats, disciples, small carousels
at your neck, my back.

When we reach the den of snakes
where the Prophet promised victory to his men,
the same den where the records say
he watched them fall
despite his chanting from behind, we are suspicious
of the wall that claims his dead
were never counted.

What beguiled us?
It's only here we find the marked trail
down, not back.
The gnats unlike disciples
cannot speak. They find our sweat.
They think the hand that breaks
their cursed procession
is not my hand.

4

NIGHT AND CHAOS

Once in the desert he said he saw
the shape of a man, a body,
the line around it neither light nor dark

standing speechless in his path.
That he could feel his shirt draw back
against his body his mind

had already given back to fear
until the figure turned to yield and let him pass
another slope of brush and rock

laid out like bodies turned in sleep,
bodies sinking in the field
that he crossed blind.

That in the desert of his mind
before the figure deemed his figure
in the dark, turned back

to wait for others crossing late behind,
he saw the room he left
at morning, the man he was

still pulling the same shirt across his chest.
That he could feel that shirt
against his skin the way

light when there is any
hope of light falls back and
back against the eye.

6 MACHISMO

Refugio from Mexico is not Mexico,
nor is every man who makes other men small
in the convex mirror of his buckle

Refugio, who turned his daughter gold
in the mirror of his own—the last world unknowable
to Refugio—the night he carried her out of Mexico

before the war to give her Mexico
before the war, before a man named *refuge*
in his native tongue could be hung from an overpass in the sun

for something smaller than his buckle:
the figures of the men unmade inside it,
the thousands vanished in its glass.

BANNER TREES

Tierra del Fuego, Argentina

Like severed arms, the hands still grasping.
Like a photograph of wind.
In my dreams of Patagonia,
the branches of the trees blown back
are stretched and braced
like open hands above a head.

The painters of the cave were in a trance.
They pressed their hands against the wall
and used a hollowed bone to blow
red paint across the backs.
The hands they left were larger than their own.
Some hands were small.

When the painting was commissioned,
when the new leader of the state
held still, the painter who once took days
to paint a tree made one hand
smaller than the other,
the olive branch a smear on his lapel.

The disappeared were drugged
then dropped from planes into the delta.
They were stripped and lined to wait
against the cabin wall.
In the dark the last to fall
saw their tied hands grow red.

They found the painter's landscapes
outside the city in a shed,
piled with other relics of the lost.
Birds had tried to make their nests
inside the painted trees.
In my dreams the trees are small.

MADE RED

At the end of the world the sun
sunk down then rolled back up
again I want to sleep but lie in bed

the television left on and don't remember
how it came to two men dressed
in the dyed wool of sheep they shear

now around the eyes and here the sheep
relent and give and fall into their hands
and see again I keep watching

these men one kneeling now
gloved at a fence and holding wire
pulled straight by some device made colder

every year outside the welding fire
that shaped it back when these men
were their fathers kneeling

on the broken stalks of a crop
passed through the animal gut
kept in flock by the wire fence

they twist in slack back over the line
with the same finesse I see their wives
knead the open end of empanadas

laid in rows and cold and waiting
for these men who know the pain
will leave their hands the way

flesh and bone can make a metal yield
but not without the hand made red
it's then I know that these

will be the last to hear the news
to wake and empty their bodies
of waste and clean and dress and knead

and still walk out to the fence
they made to keep the animals away
from the animals we made.

WINDFALL

and overhead up grew . . .
Cedar, and pine, and fir, and branching palm.
—PARADISE LOST

We lived by the rich and thought we were rich.
Mornings we walked by rows of cypresses
and missed their shadows in our gait. We saw
men raise a hundred towers dressed like pines
that never grew. The way we knew a false
pine from the true was how it moved in wind.
At night we heard speakers in the false pines
hum, then cue, but no one spoke. We slept by
each other and thought we slept. In our dreams
the palms were leaning in the wind, straining
to hear. The cypresses confused our gaits.
But each time we woke, the towers shook more
like pines. Their needles grew. Soon all the palms
were signing *wind*. But no one braced for wind.

How did the bird get inside the house?
Through the door I said.
No. Through a window. Listen they said How did the
bird get inside the house?
Through a window I said.
No. Through the chimney. How did it get inside?
Through the chimney I said.
It hatched inside. Who named the bird?
A child. A child named it.
The bird is nameless. Who named the bird?
I said No one. The bird is nameless.
What is your name? they said.
I am nameless I said.
Yes they said.

THE OATH

They took the first card
that marked her *alien*
when she answered
"Declaration." When she knew
the names of statues
they took her fingerprints
and weighed her. Then they took
her from her children
to ask her questions,
take her picture. I watched her
when she stood in line
with others taking turns
reciting words to make them
citizens. Some were taken
out to smaller rooms
before their turn. Some returned.
In the oath my mother
cleared her throat before
a word then said the word,
made the same sound
I knew to listen for
when I had lost her in a crowd,

in the aisles of a store.
The sound was louder
than the oath. It meant
her lungs were still shaped
by thirty years of foreign air
despite the vow that made her
one of us. They took
her country when she spoke,
but the cords that first
learned Spanish in her throat
spoke first: last strain of loss
and its resistance.

What is beautiful about the Iranian boy
who dips his fingers in the river,
who is blind, who reads the stones there,
is that he translates what he finds
for no one. I may be wrong.
                                                It was,
after all, a film I hardly remember,
a boy reading braille in the riverbed.
Once in a school meeting common
to the inner city, I was called to interpret
for a Mexican father.
                                        The Board, raised
on a platform, sat before us sipping
water. They had closed his son's school.
I remember that I barely knew the man's
Spanish; that he, at last, kept none of his
anger back; but also that
                                                when he stopped
speaking—my turn to translate his words—
I was confused at first, simply
started back in Spanish with what he asked.
The father laughed; the Board followed.
The room of parents broke
                                                into laughter.

I keep that sound like the words I offer
no one; buried stones I find weeding
the garden; the word my young
son speaks who finds me there, points
to sweat on my forehead, says *water*.

COAX

It was easy to worship obedient things.
The water that fell off
their heads made pools

on the floor. The shape it left
changed according to the head
immersed. In the shower

I let water run down my arm
a small river convinced
I felt the first realized ache.

When the river knew the shape of my arm
better than the arm I knew
by sight, I knew water

poured over a face would reveal that face
likewise. When I coaxed my enemy
to speak with water,

when I showed how the uncoaxed thing
behaves, it was always language
I was after. Names.

AUSTRAL

Name for what we never name above:
Far south. Farther. Land of light
that goes out slow. Land of

prisons without doors. Land of fire.
Some say the angels God cast down
fell for an age. From here

we use our palms to blot the sun.
The prisoners we send south
soon lose their names. The young

their sight. The sun grows old.
Still, when it dies, not even distance
will keep the land of fire cold.

When she cut the rattle—
its sound
like the dive and swell
of infants
squealing in a chapel, writhing
under pews—
the snake grew still,
then grew
like a swollen branch that darkens
in the rain,
dries, shrinks back
into its shape,
made new, made straight.

THE FALL

She disappeared, and left me dark.
—PARADISE LOST

1

Small rain on the lake,
its glacial blue. Last at the tail
of a continental range.
I followed you until the trail

grew too arduous to climb
without a stick. All rock
along the border of two countries
whose only war was which

still had the farthest city south.
The sticks we used kept snapping
in the roots. I found a branch
too heavy for the climb,

bare except a spiral knot.
You took it by the throat,
left me behind. I watched the knot
turn back into an eye.

2

That night I woke
and pulled the bed sheet back
to see the wound,
how the first bruise in dark

still blue beneath your naked foot
grew lines to others
like a trail of every rock
you broke against

cast in the half-light of the room.
In that dark I saw you climbing
over rock again, the yellow stakes
still bright against the trail.

When you turned I watched
the straight branch break in two:
one half still standing in the rock
where you fell.

3

That morning when I took our sons
outside, made each hold
the corners of a sheet
and pull it taut

to teach what I learned young
of gravity and constant fall,
in that moment
when they watched a heavy ball

sink down a star
into the bed sheet's heart,
pull lesser weights toward it
in a curve, I thought

I saw you naked underneath,
alone, but now the swollen veins
had made your bruise a sun
to other wounds and other men.

Then the woman who couldn't sleep
for the ache inside her ear,
who lit every light bulb in her house
until the glare outside was bright enough
to change the weather in her neighbor's dream,
who reached up and pulled down a bulb
each time the glass of one
she laid against her ear grew cold
emptied of its light, and who waited
until she had drained each one—
the day changed back to night
behind her neighbor's eyes—
for the deep ache to leave, couldn't sleep
for the tips of her fingers burning.

MOUTH

La vida es una cueva, la muerte es el espacio.
—ALFONSINA STORNI

What other prayer
but shut the lion's mouth?
When those who crawl
in caves too tortuous

to hold them
can't crawl back, who push
until their limbs unfold,
what is left to pray for?

The mouth is closed around them.
When a man stopped breathing
in the "Birth Canal,"
when the rescuers left him

where it closed, rolled stones
over the cave's mouth,
no other prayer but one:
In the morning,

the scripture goes, the king
called for Daniel; Daniel,
from the closed mouth, spoke:
O *king, live for ever.*

If the rib cage is a labyrinth
for the heart,

if the saws
that split cadavers hang
from cords,
retractable string,

then the heart,
like the cursed half-beast waiting
at the heart,
is not the first thing

feared:
even the saws pulled back in dust
a rib cage makes.

When I reached the chapel
in a house of God
empty of its smoke,

when I passed the rooms
around it, the doors
that opened into

the rooms,
the dark, the hallways straight,
I still recoiled.

I thought that the heart was safe;
that the cages

meant to keep it safe
could still amaze.

Then the river
I hadn't found

held ransom the rivers
I had. I knew

I wouldn't find it.
I would leave

where I wanted
to stay. I was

convinced we pay
no other price.

Then the river
I hadn't found

held *everything* I had.
The way belief

holds proof
so we forget.

I could hear
the sound of water.

I thought
it didn’t matter

if I never found
what made it,

until I left.

DYSTOCIA

Sometimes a myth
delivers its prophet

breech. The room is quiet
up to the neck,

then the head
comes out speaking.

Sometimes a myth is
delivered by forceps,

broken clavicle, the bones
scarred by many births,

the scars tracks of cavalcades,
migrants crossing.

Rigoberto Salas-López, 30, was charged with transporting illegal immigrants resulting in death. Eight of the 14 people in the Chevy Suburban died after it rolled several times on U.S. 191 a few hours before dawn Monday. Salas-López, originally from Guatemala, told investigators he swerved to miss a horse. He was arrested after fleeing into the desert in the Four Corners area of Utah, New Mexico, Arizona, and Colorado.

—ASSOCIATED PRESS, APRIL 17, 2007

The passengers say no, he wasn't swerving to miss a horse, that he was fondling a female passenger in the front seat of the vehicle.

—SERGEANT RICK ELDREDGE
IN THE SALT LAKE TRIBUNE

1

Say it was a horse.
That the horse watched
the three-ton van

roll until it stopped
where their bodies
stopped. That the horse

unlike a horse waited
until he stood. Say it was
the horse he followed

in the desert. Say it was
the desert, the sagebrush
that kept the horse. Say

it was the trail he left
the patrolmen followed.
That they never found

the horse. That he covered
the horse tracks in
the desert with his own.

2

The sergeant doesn't find the wreckage first. When he asks the survivors how many cars passed in the desert three hours before morning, they tell him they remember only one, that someone moved the bodies from the road and drove away. In their language they say this road is a river nothing gathers. The sergeant asks to see their driver and one points to the desert. The rest point to the woman he reached for: a hole the body left passing through the windshield.

3

Son,
in Spanish you do not agree,
you must *be in agreement,*
estar de acuerdo.

Two people may agree or disagree,
like we do,
but they must also *be* in one
or the other.

If you mistake

cuerdo for
cuerda

you will have said *rope*
or *cord,*
though both words divide and bind
some older form of

agreement.

As a boy I saw
a model of the spinal cord,
how the nerves run down,
divide us behind.

They named it *cauda equina*—
horse tail—buried
cord.

4

In his dream the sergeant takes a shovel to the river to hold the river back. He is told he will find nothing, to keep nothing he finds. The sergeant stands in the river until his feet freeze, until they lose their hold, until it is the shovel itself he holds to keep from slipping under. The river is choked with debris. It is a bird's nest, finally, that passes, convincing him. Inside he sees small branches woven, then string, then needles, clothing, then hair. He untangles the nest to braid a rope.

5

Say the three names
he gave the sergeant
were true. Say

the names of the
eight bodies pulled from
the wreckage became

the numbers they first
labeled them by. Say
the eighth is no longer

nameless. Say they still
tie ropes to the caskets
of immigrants they find

in the desert. That a rope
saves time should
someone come looking.

Say they bury the ropes
for the dead to climb
back. Say their names.

6

Son, do not mistake

cabello for
caballo,

hair for
horse,

that *caballero,*
though *gentleman,*
meant

horseman.

You've heard the Spanish
conquered Mexico
on their horses.

You've heard the conquered
could not tell
the man from horse
and ask me

How do we know
the conquered knew?

They listened. The horses
never spoke.

BEGET

Only one who draws the knife gets Isaac.
—KIERKEGAARD

Then three paused: a baby
and his father; his mother with a knife
still in her hand, in the father.
It was the color that startled the baby,
the mother, the knife.
They were cooking before the father
turned himself into the knife,
the dinner they made spilling over.

Then three moved quickly: the mother
turned to catch her baby; the father
reached to turn the burner; but the baby
could only see as one sees color
from a window, reached for what the father
had turned into, the knife.

though neither owned it,
how it killed the son
    and not the father
    who followed,

who fought thereafter
as his son. Returned. Lost
    his wife to those
    who kept her

in his absence,
though he knew it
    when he left.
    Who slept with women

younger than his son then,
women with whom
    he spoke little
    of the war

and how the war aged
everyone but those
    who fought it—
    the hair grown

back out of baldness,
the weight shorn off
in sweat.
Who saw age

rinse from his face
like stains from the cover
of his pillow,
its laundered case.

Who knew that war
like age still left
its circles
when he slept.

ONCE

They put the terrorist's face on each urinal cake
in the fourteen-screen cineplex
men's room. Someone crossed out *Men,*
wrote *Target Practice.* Soon a line

we couldn't see the end of curled back
inside the theater door. We heard a curse
each time more reached the lobby, blinking.
Inside, fathers held their boys up to the bowl.

Some laughed. No one could avoid the face.
We tried. Some shook as if it all came back.
Some gasped instead of sighed. Then each man

in front saw those who finished stumble backward
to their theater door; heard them curse,
blame the line; watched the film reverse.

MAR

After the war disfigured
they gave men effigies of their faces
cast by sculptors.

They took sculptors
who learned first
to mar,

that ruin
always precedes art,
and gave them soldiers.

Soldiers they taught first to mar
effigies of men
were given sculptors.

PROSTHETIC

Damned by an amateur's gun. The buckshot
that took one eye of the young watercolorist

took also his genius. Therefore he taught
middle school children to paint, to cut

bound stock of construction paper with that
flat ruled blade he feared would carve their

clumsy fingers. But the brutish children
who mocked him, who sat where his dark,

prosthetic eye could not see them,
were never clumsy. That day they spilled ketchup

and pretended to mangle their hands
in the cutter, it was his bellow at the sight

and not their cunning that made their false cries true,
gave the real cry its urgent measure.

The others turned from their tables and listened.
The teacher rinsed the ruined hands

under the spout of running water
until that red had leaked into the other

discarded colors, unwashed brushes, mixed
in that massive sink stained black around the drain.

The children held their hands as if they bled.
No one looking knew their blood from paint.

ÁNGEL

A messenger's name for a boy
who spoke one language of violence
and no other well.

Your parents stayed late
in the English class my parents taught,
and we corralled

in the school that was our hell,
broke into the halls
and waited to be found.

Then rooms I knew only by one light
I saw altered by another:
the locker room empty

of its sweat, still life of the stalls
we changed behind instead,
the rust-choked shower heads

that never reached the blood along one wall.
I knew your boredom
where others knew force,

saw the same tremor in your hand
I watched your father hide
late from work.

They called our names
when class was over. *Ángel—*
your mother's voice was small

but steady in the dark,
convinced the sound would reach
her son, that she could keep one

word the same. *Espérame—*
your voice would come.
Wait for me.

Always from the bushes, burdened, five or six
unshaven, their shoes white with sawdust. Before
Aggie saw need to call I'd set to laying

chairs across the lawn. Never heard them speak. Not
to me. When they'd sit and Aggie brought and filled
for each a jar of water, I'd stay to sweep

the grass my boots tracked in the kitchen, kneel at
the window, watch the glasses shake at their lips
before the water fell in. And sometimes I

was angry at that. Thought thirsty men wouldn't
waste their water or let it fall and rinse their
shoes like that. Then they'd leave. Once I asked Aggie

to let me leave the chairs outside, the jars just
where the men left them—I'd take them in before
dark—and she agreed. But I forgot until

morning, woke to Aggie old and dragging chairs
inside her kitchen, still wet by my mistake,
raking in the cold, soaked grass I couldn't sweep.

Always from the bushes, burdened, two or three
unshaven, their shoes blurred by ashes. Before
Aggie saw need to call I'd set to laying

chairs across the lawn. Never heard them speak. Not
to me. When they'd sit and Aggie filled for each
a jar of water, I'd stay to sweep the grass

my boots tracked in the kitchen, kneel and listen
at the window until the heavy glasses
shaking at their lips grew still. And sometimes I

grew angry at that, at the way God saw need
to clothe his ministers in rags, the same God
who once gave prophets staffs to curse a boulder

for the water underneath. Then they'd leave. Once
in boldness after Aggie made me leave her
chairs outside, the jars just where the men left them,

her sign to God she'd host again, I went out
in the dark while she slept to drag it all back
in. Then I drank each glass the dew refilled clean.

My father wakes his sons to move pipe
lift from the center he says
the equal weight on either side
bright morning smell of pollen
or the crop we're sent to
water sometimes the pipes
still have water so Gabby
the oldest lifts one by the center
behind my father pours
the heavy water down his back cold
across his shoulders and his cry is
primal deepest shock

In the bus station already erased by
exhaust the idling engines
of Mar del Plata we are leaving
everyone my mother left in Argentina
before she married my father
Jorge her first love first
to see us off is lifting a suitcase
into the bus turns it on its side
then looks back to help my father

with another and his face
his cry the same his shock
we didn't know the pipe had water
we couldn't lift it up

56

JORGE, FIRST LOVE OF MY ARGENTINE MOTHER

In the '86 Renault you drove
from the sea to Tandil,
on the beltless front-seat bar

between you and my American father,
I slept but could not dream.
When I woke it was as one wakes to voices

aware of others sleeping in the car,
but no one was speaking.
We were the only two awake.

When you spoke you sounded like a man ignored,
one orphan speaking to another
who was not.

I knew only what they told me:
She couldn't love you back.
That you married her sister, Alba, when she left

and raised your sons in Mar del Plata
miles from that coast and crowded sand.
That once along some shoreline road

you lost your brakes,
turned and rolled the first Renault you drove in '76.
That crawling out alone

you tried to free my mother's legs
still pinned between the seat and frame.
That my father, unseen from the car that ran behind,

found my mother's head and arms
and pulled her from the other side
until she screamed—

We could have torn her at the waist.
She chose what she could see:
kicked until your hands let go.

I think it was the bar not meant
to hold a child that woke me.
How it rattled first and then grew hot

beneath our weight.
Or the narrow air inside the car,
the '86 not meant to carry those passengers:

Susana, Alba, and Abuela in the back,
my father buried in his snore.
Or the road despite its track through open pampas

not cut straight, that drew the length
between the sea and Tandil.
I think it was your question about distance in my ear.

What would the prison cook who made the rapist's last meal cook finally for himself? What could it matter that from his window he looked like other men who rinsed their hands in dishwater? That even before he ate he filled the sink until the water burned his fingers. A rag laid out for drying. The steam stumbling from *a train south of Mar del Plata, a girl sleeps again without wishing to, wakes to an arm that pulls her through a door into Miramar, blinks beside the man who woke her, not her father, though to others he looks as though he were a man with his daughter, the daughter does not speak, only cries when later, in a restaurant, he gives her a menu she cannot read and makes her order* his plate like a catalogue of every meal that could have filled it. How when he felt it right to kneel beside the table, give thanks, the words swelled in his mouth as if he spoke them in a barrel, like a victim must with little choice left but where to rest her hands.

How many would it take?
Ropes?

Must take hundreds.
One.

Must take hundreds.
You don't know that.

What?
That he didn't still feel it.

Don't you?
What do you think?

I think a burn is different from a callus.
Not for him.

But he was burned.
Don't make a story of it.

A son says *this is my kingdom.*
His father sees the play, says
this is my kingdom. Already

the son is pointing where
their kingdoms meet.
But where the father looks he sees

only poor in the boy's kingdom:
a cemetery cleared
of headstones for the poor

to make gardens, a mother
who pulled out bones
with her potatoes

assuring her daughter the bones
once made a horse.
The father sees the girl

assemble the bones into figures,
dress them in potato skins.
They are headless. They guard

her kingdom. Some have shoots
growing from their eyes.
The father sees the mother

remake the same small hole
with her hands. He confuses repetition
for digging. The father says

there are only poor in your kingdom.
The son forgets
what *kingdom* means.

THE LESION

All this to say my father kept
an orchard of peaches,

that it never went unnoticed
from the roadway: the rows of trees

appeared as rows. That we had to step
outside their pattern for the peach lost in gathering

to see the rows as knots.
I could say that order

hides disorder, that any witness of disorder
is not a witness. But the peach

always rotted where it fell.
We knew the violet bruise was just

one lesion of its rot. If we saw
our father pull his sleeve to wrist,

we turned away,
knew to act like we had not.

SMALL BLOOD

Morning, bowl, small
blood

in the egg yolk.
It meant winter—

nests
like tumors

in the trees.
In this tumor, this

nest, a tree.
Winter,

nest, egg whites
strained from yolk

instead—
the tree

will not stop
blooming.

God knows why the boy
forces his body each morning through the space where two
chain-link fences meet

outside my window.
I say *God* because I have watched him make some crude sign of the cross
before his trespass there.

One arm raised above his head,
then down again. What made me cross that hallowed space
the day June's

straight-line winds
blew out my bedroom windows, what made me stay
despite the storm,

kept me dry
under the blossomed halves of maples stripped for power lines,
was the same lucky stupor

that thought those trees
a symbol of the brain: branched and leafy one side,
barren on the other,

the heavy wires taut in space.
I dreamed that men would come back late with ladders while I slept,
climb where the wind

had snapped a line
of telephone poles in half, repair the masts still hanging by their wires,
not replace.

But something stopped me
at the gate: a cobweb laced between the fence posts,
the strands still wet with rain.

I broke it with my arm
held straight, passed through. Knew what he knew.
We would make that sign again.

ROUND

State departments of transportation often use military artillery to control the avalanche threat. Occasionally the ordnance does not explode upon impact: a potential risk to hikers after the snow melts.

—UNITED STATES FOREST SERVICE

1

All night the sound of water
in a ditch. No dreams to speak of.

Not the cannon shells
across the canyon or their routine

sound. Snow
pulled from the mountain like a sleeve

torn from a shoulder.
We inoculate our son. In the needle,

the same virus we hope his body
will defeat.

2

In my father's dream
it is the ditch that wakes him,

All night the sound of water
in a ditch. No dreams to speak of

voices coming from the lawn.
Outside, men stand with their arms uncrossed,

Not the cannon shells
across the canyon or their routine

men who ask him for his boots.
When he slips them from his feet

sound. Snow
pulled from the mountain

he sees water spilling from the tops,
water running from the porch

torn from a shoulder.
We inoculate our son. In the needle

and gutter, water where the ditch had been,
the mountains all made low

the same virus we hope his body
will defeat

3

I woke, waited
barefoot by my window

In my father's dream
it is the ditch

until the cannon shook my roof again,
sent the smallest avalanche

coming from the lawn.
Outside

it had not meant to
barreling from my shingles.

his boots.
When he slips them from his feet

In the dream
I saw men standing where the ditch had been,

water spilling from the tops,
running

then only half
their bodies stranded in the snow

where the ditch had been,
the mountains all made low

4

When they said it was a boy
hiked farther than the others on the mountain,

woke, waited
barefoot by my window

stumbled on the live round
in the grass and pine needles where the shell

shook my roof again
the smallest avalanche

struck in winter,
I dreamed I also picked the metal from the ground

had not meant to
barreling

to see it better,
knew its risk by weight alone,

In the dream
I saw men standing

ran the shell back quickly
to my father

then only half
their bodies stranded in the snow

5

When they said it was a boy
hiked farther than the others on the mountain,

stumbled on the live round
in the grass and pine needles where the shell

struck in winter,
I dreamed I also picked the metal from the ground

to see it better,
knew its risk by weight alone,

ran the shell back quickly
to my father.

Say it was a man.
It was. There is
a boy mowing

the cemetery lawn.
He is perfect
at cutting close.

Go in. How will I know
when it's close?
The ground

unpacked above his box
remade the box
above the ground.

Sit down. Say he sat down.
Where? It matters
that they sat so close.

How many? Fourteen.
Make room. The mower
stops to move a vase.

The sweetest dream
that labor knows. His space
marked at the gate—

UNKNOWN MALE.
What could he do
in the van without space?

Say he was sleeping.
Did he dream? Yes.
And after the crash?

Died in the dream.
Inside. Or woke
in the sand. The brush.

The ground was his dream.
Legs pulled up in a van
dream of ground.

Under now. Wake up,
the mower says.
He has stopped

where I lie. His face.
You have aged, I say.
Wake up.

I am looking up.
Will you still age?
His face is changed.

GALLOP

Because the lever is archaic that pulls
this horse into gallop—it is my son's best
picture book—I will mend the page

he tore, bend the torn horse back,
the break that one side kept and where
the other gave way, cover the machinery

of the page, the window, the illusion
of lined acetate film pulled over
this horse, this gallop, sketched

and disembodied in every possible
frame. It was Muybridge, after all,
who proved that horses tuck their legs

beneath them when they run, that in one
blurred gesture all their hooves
leave the ground—whose cameras

gave way to moving pictures.
But I've already seen the lever draw back
the tape. I know what makes the horse

arc in place, who holds the mended page,
who still thinks the horse retreats
when its broken legs fall back.

The kite string I unraveled
for my brothers, hiking,
cast our way back.

We climbed out of order:
the youngest ahead,
skinny, short as the sagebrush

he slipped between; the oldest
in center, weightlifter,
listening. The story

wasn't mine, but when I spoke
I couldn't feel the hiking.
Beneath us what had cut

the canyon was also out
of order: railway, freeway, river.
Three mixed like twine

beginning to unspell.
I must have loved the story:
horses spoke, kept sacred names.

My older brother
put the youngest between us.
We reached the oldest sheets

of snow. They stopped climbing
when I forgot, waited,
kept on when I spoke.

The string spun out—
I could see my brothers hiking,
one sometimes passing

the other. Soon they grew older.
Their faces wore the same
but would not become

each other, the way two
mountains rise the same way
out a canyon and do not meet

again. They climbed because
my tongue spoke behind them
in the story. The canyon

was a mouth. My brothers
turned back: the three roads
became an artery,

the white tongue lost in snow.
Soon one trembled, both cold,
until the other put his ear

low, listened—I listened—
horses spoke. Kept sacred names.
The older always put the younger

behind, followed those names,
their making, down—which was
in—until my bright mouth closed.

"In fables . . ."
Prophet's Rock can still be found near Battle Ground, Indiana, site of the Battle of Tippecanoe. The "Prophet" mentioned is Tenskwatawa, brother of Tecumseh. Tenskwatawa's given name was Lalawethika, or "the rattle."

"Night and Chaos"
In *Paradise Lost*, both are figures who greet Satan outside the gates of Hell on his journey to this new world.

"Windfall"
The first line is inspired by a statement made by the mayor of San Jose when he was asked about California's fiscal crisis in an article published by *Vanity Fair*.

"Austral"
The name of an Argentine domestic airline serving Tierra del Fuego.

"Mouth"
In memory of John Jones.

"'. . . as Saint Mark says they mustn't'"
The title of this poem is derived from a phrase in Robert Frost's "Directive."

86 "The Ground"

This poem borrows from Robert Frost's "Mowing" and is dedicated to the unknown male in an unmarked plot at Blanding City Cemetery, San Juan County, Utah, "the eighth" victim mentioned in "Caballero."

With gratitude to the editors of the following publications in which these poems, some in different versions, first appeared: *Adroit Journal, Beloit Poetry Journal, Boston Review, Colorado Review, Crab Orchard Review, FIELD, Hayden's Ferry Review, Huizache, Image, Indiana Review, Mid-American Review, New Madrid, The New Yorker, The Paris-American, Poet Lore, Poetry, Rattle, Smartish Pace, Third Coast,* and *Weber.*

"The Lesion" appeared in the anthology *Time You Let Me In: 25 Poets under 25* (edited by Naomi Shihab Nye, Greenwillow Books, 2010); "Gallop" was reprinted in *PN Review* (UK).

My deepest thanks to the MFA Program in Creative Writing at Purdue University, the Creative Writing Program at Stanford University, the Unterberg Poetry Center at the 92nd Street Y, and The Westminster Schools for their generous support of my work and these poems in particular

To Jim Schley, Marie Gauthier, Jeffrey Levine, and everyone at Tupelo Press: What an extraordinary gift.

To my teachers, for their patience and sacrifice: Brad Roghaar, Don Platt, Mary Leader, Wendy Flory, Ken Fields, Eavan Boland, and Simone Di Piero. To Naomi Shihab Nye, Robert Wrigley, and Jericho Brown, for renewing my hope. To Marianne Boruch, who called very late one night and changed everything. And to Robert Pinsky for his choice.

To my friends and the many early readers of these poems: You are also my teachers, and I am fortunate to be in your company.

To my family, from this country to el fin del mundo. To those who live in these poems: my parents and my siblings. To my sons—there are clues here if you search for them. And to Wendy, for our life together, and how we once stood like *the nameless who first brought her young / to the shore, / looked down into the water, / shapeless: city / without form.*

OTHER BOOKS FROM TUPELO PRESS

Silver Road: Essays, Maps & Calligraphies (hybrid memoir), Kazim Ali

A Certain Roughness in Their Syntax (poems), Jorge Aulicino, translated by Judith Filc

Another English: Anglophone Poems from Around the World (anthology), edited by Catherine Barnett and Tiphanie Yanique

Personal Science (poems), Lillian-Yvonne Bertram

Everything Broken Up Dances (poems), James Byrne

New Cathay: Contemporary Chinese Poetry (anthology), edited by Ming Di

Rapture & the Big Bam (poems), Matt Donovan

Calazazza's Delicious Dereliction (poems), Suzanne Dracius, translated by Nancy Naomi Carlson

Hallowed: Selected and New Poems (poems), Patricia Fargnoli

Gossip and Metaphysics: Russian Modernist Poetry and Prose (anthology), edited by Katie Farris, Ilya Kaminsky, and Valzhyna Mort

The Posthumous Affair (novel), James Friel

Poverty Creek Journal (memoir), Thomas Gardner

Leprosarium (poems), Lise Goett

My Immaculate Assassin (novel), David Huddle

Darktown Follies (poems), Amaud Jamaul Johnson

A God in the House: Poets Talk About Faith (interviews), edited by Ilya Kaminsky and Katherine Towler

Third Voice (poems), Ruth Ellen Kocher

The Cowherd's Son (poems), Rajiv Mohabir

Marvels of the Invisible (poems), Jenny Molberg

Canto General: Song of the Americas (poems), Pablo Neruda, translated by Mariela Griffor and Jeffrey Levine

Lucky Fish (poems), Aimee Nezhukumatathil

Ex-Voto (poems), Adélia Prado, translated by Ellen Doré Watson

Why Don't We Say What We Mean? (essays), Lawrence Raab

Intimate: An American Family Photo Album (hybrid memoir), Paisley Rekdal

Thrill-Bent (novel), Jan Richman

The Voice of That Singing (poems), Juliet Rodeman

Dirt Eaters (poems), Eliza Rotterman

Walking Backwards (poems), Lee Sharkey

Good Bones (poems), Maggie Smith

Service (poems), Grant Souders

Swallowing the Sea (essays), Lee Upton

Butch Geography (poems), Stacey Waite

See our complete list at www.tupelopress.org